EDDIE VAN HALEN | GUITAR VIRTU...

Includes 9 Classic Solo Guitar Instrumentals

Cover photo: © Neil Zlozower

Alfred Publishing Co., Inc.
16320 Roscoe Blvd., Suite 100
P.O. Box 10003
Van Nuys, CA 91410-0003
alfred.com

ISBN-10: 0-7390-4494-X
ISBN-13: 978-0-7390-4494-0

CONTENTS

ALBUM INDEX

316

Music by
SAMMY HAGAR, EDWARD VAN HALEN,
ALEX VAN HALEN and MICHAEL ANTHONY

316 - 21 - 1

*Tapped harmonics. Fret note normally and
tap at fret indicated in parentheses.

6

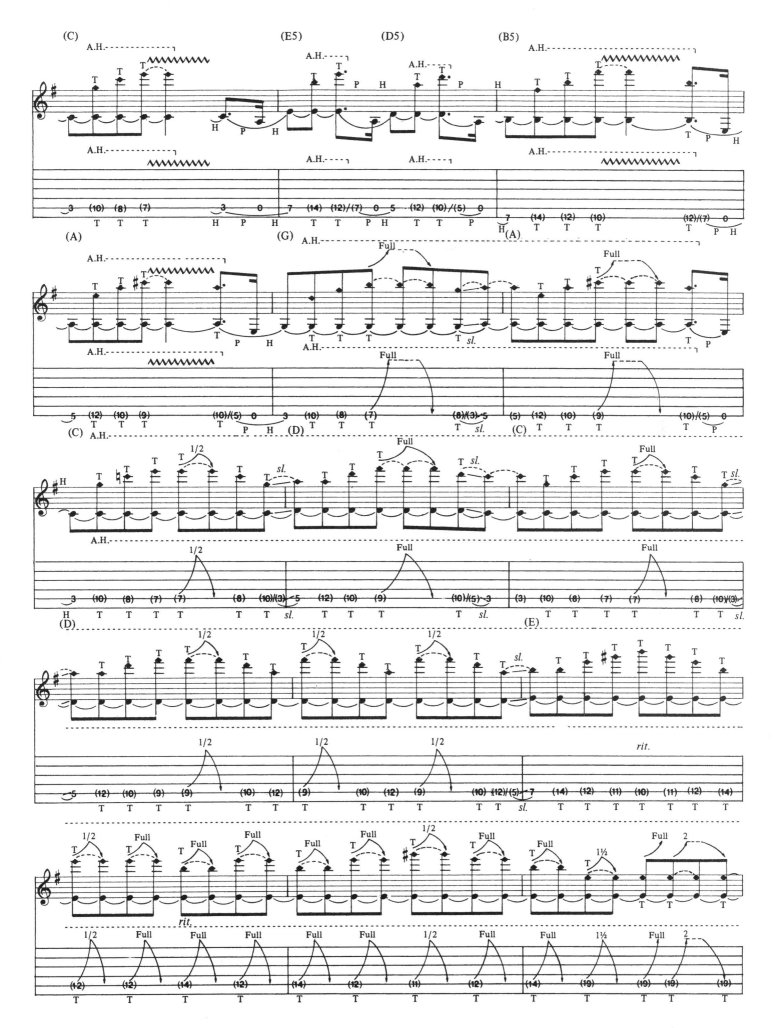

BALUCHITHERIUM

Music by
SAMMY HAGAR, EDWARD VAN HALEN,
ALEX VAN HALEN and MICHAEL ANTHONY

*Drop D-tuning: ⑥ = D   *Chords implied by bass (next 8 bars only).

*Execute bend w/L.H. middle finger and bend stg. towards floor.
At beat 3 ½, hammer on at 5th fr. w/L.H. ring finger while stg. is still bent.

*Bend w/middle finger as before.

Baluchitherium - 12 - 1

30

*Chords implied by bass (next 8 bars only).

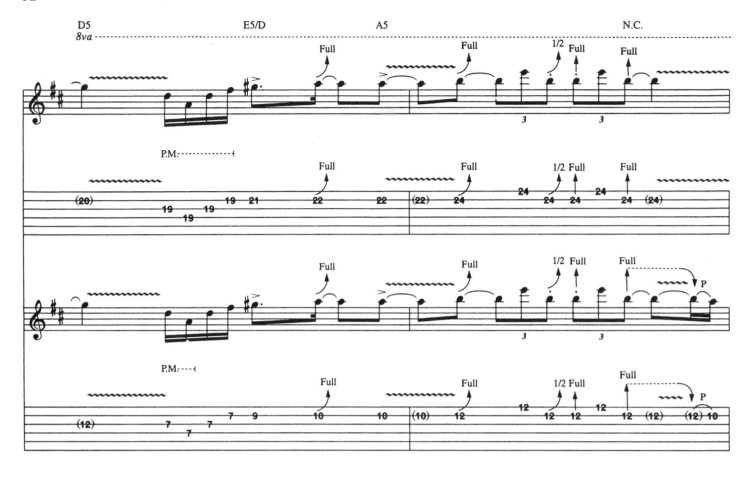

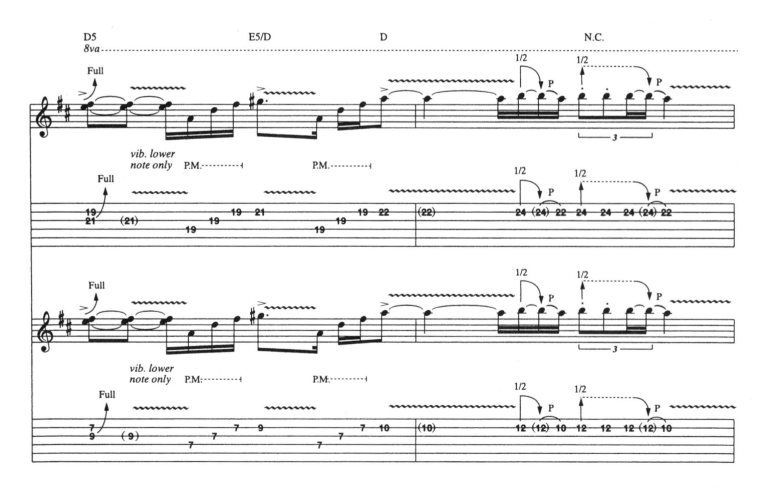

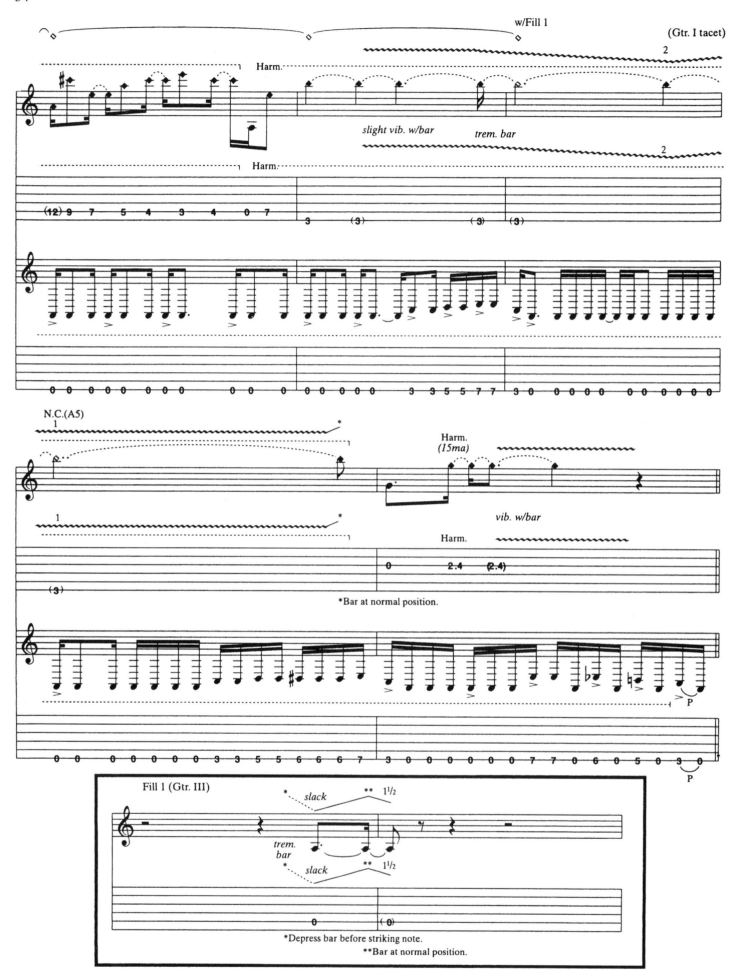

LITTLE GUITARS (INTRO)

Music by
EDWARD VAN HALEN, ALEX VAN HALEN,
MICHAEL ANTHONY and DAVID LEE ROTH

*Music sounds one whole step higher than written because
capo is placed at 2nd fret. Tab numbers are relative to capo.

Segue to LITTLE GUITARS

CATHEDRAL

Music by
EDWARD VAN HALEN, ALEX VAN HALEN,
MICHAEL ANTHONY and DAVID LEE ROTH

Cathedral - 2 - 1

ERUPTION

Music by
EDWARD VAN HALEN, ALEX VAN HALEN,
MICHAEL ANTHONY and DAVID LEE ROTH

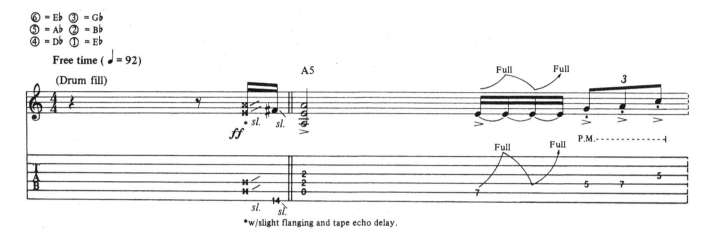

*w/slight flanging and tape echo delay.

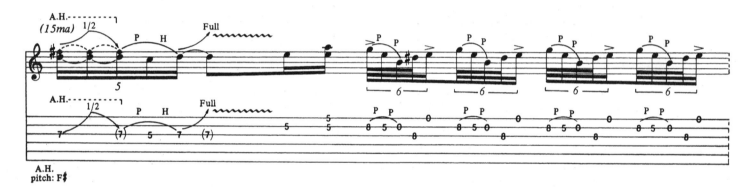

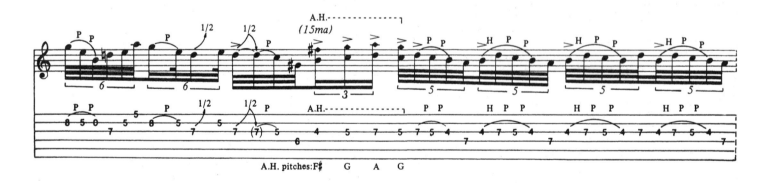

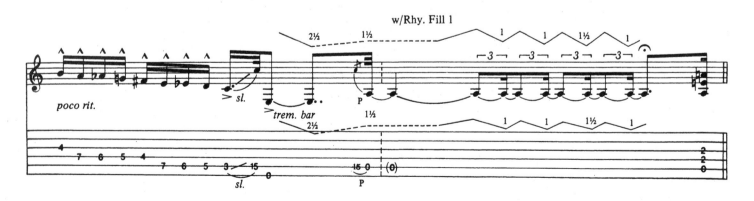

Eruption - 4 - 1

*Release finger pressure when arriving at 19fr. at end of slide to sound F# natural harmonic.

Rhy. Fill 1

Overdubbed gtr.

42

*Slightly rushed.

*Tap open low E at 12fr. to produce octave harmonic.   Fdbk. pitch: B

(Echoplex on)

trem. bar
rit.

dim. **w/tape echo effect.

**Univox tape echo runaway feedback effect.

Eruption - 4 - 4

NEWORLD

Music by
EDWARD VAN HALEN, ALEX VAN HALEN,
MICHAEL ANTHONY and GARY CHERONE

Tune Down: ⑥ = D.

Moderately slow, in 1 ♩. = 46

Intro:
freely

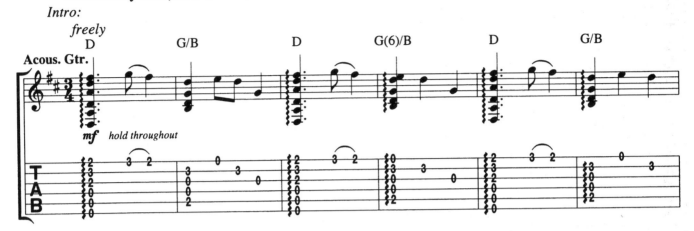

Faster ♩. = 50
Main Theme:

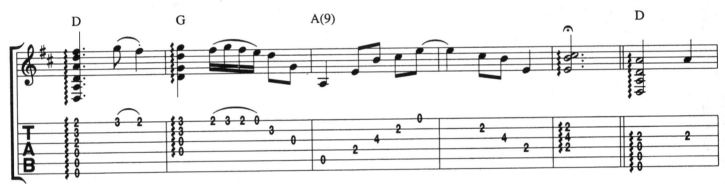

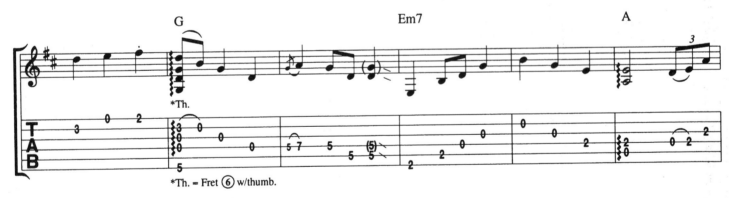

*Th. = Fret ⑥ w/thumb.

Neworld - 3 - 1

*Chords played by keybd.

SPANISH FLY

Music by
EDWARD VAN HALEN, ALEX VAN HALEN,
MICHAEL ANTHONY and DAVID LEE ROTH

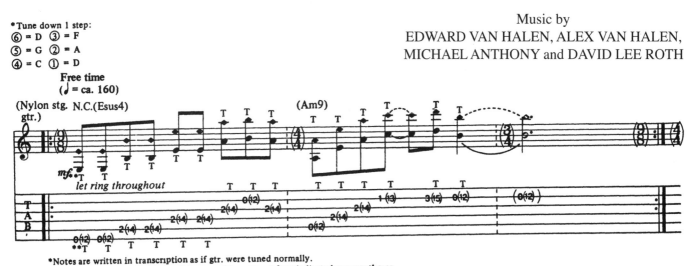

*Notes are written in transcription as if gtr. were tuned normally.
**Tapped harmonics. Hold chord forms and tap stgs. at frets indicated in parentheses.

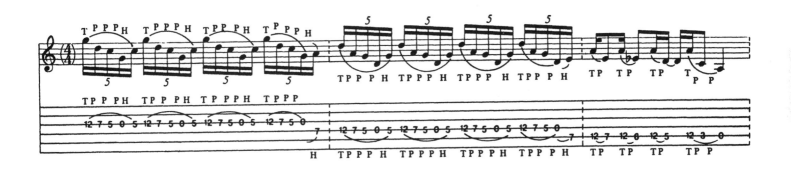

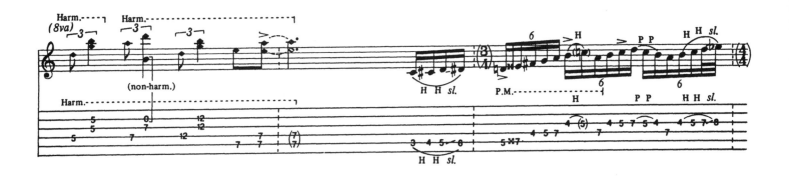

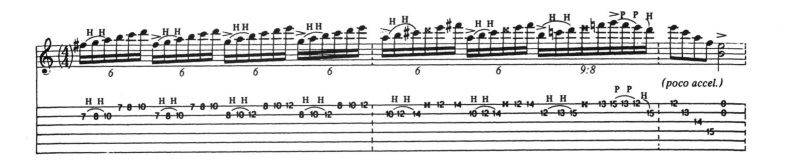

Spanish Fly - 3 - 1

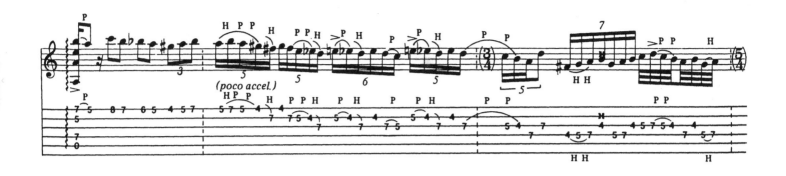

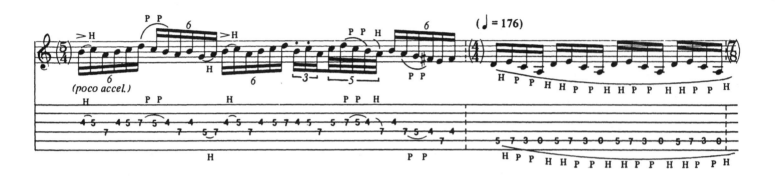

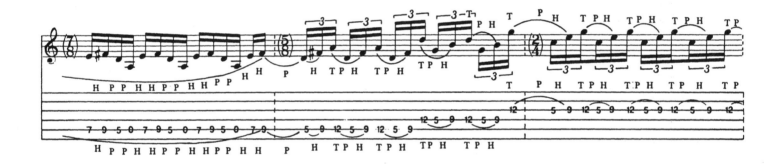

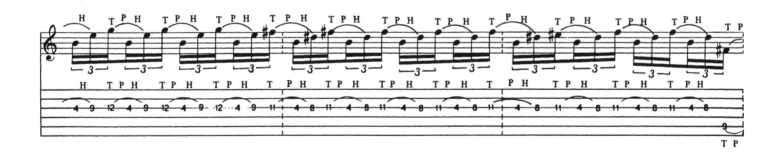

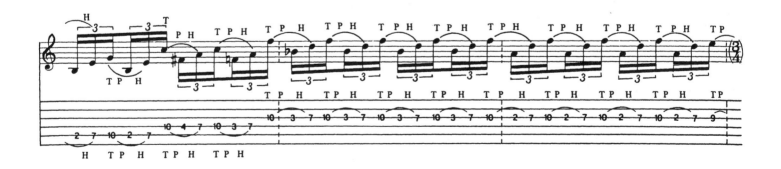

50

PRIMARY

Music by
EDWARD VAN HALEN, ALEX VAN HALEN,
MICHAEL ANTHONY and GARY CHERONE

Gtr.1 in open A tuning w/low A:

⑥– A*   ③– A
⑤– A   ②– C#
④– E   ①– E

* ⑥ A is 1 octave lower than ⑤ A.

Free time (♩ = 76, approx.)

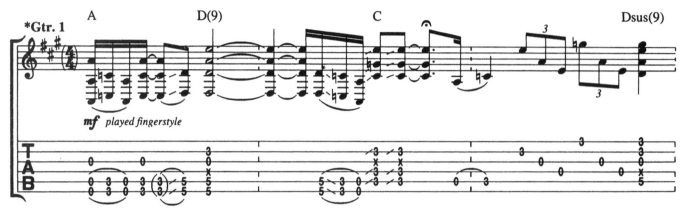

*Gtr. 1 is a Coral electric sitar arr. for standard gtr.

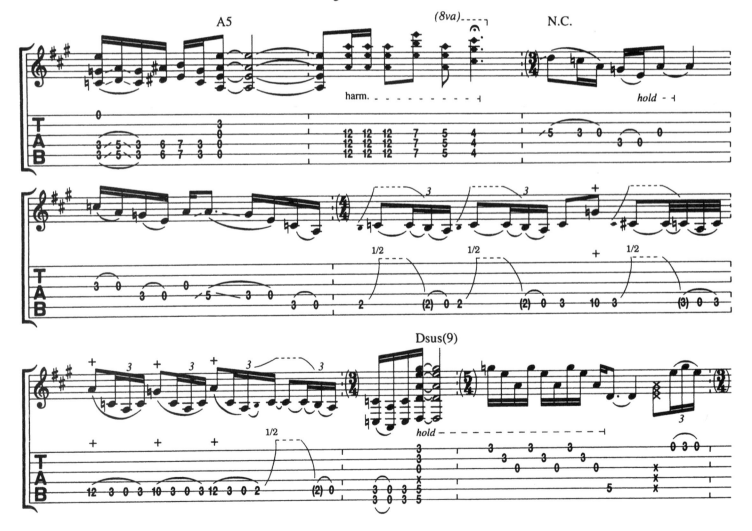

Primary - 2 - 1

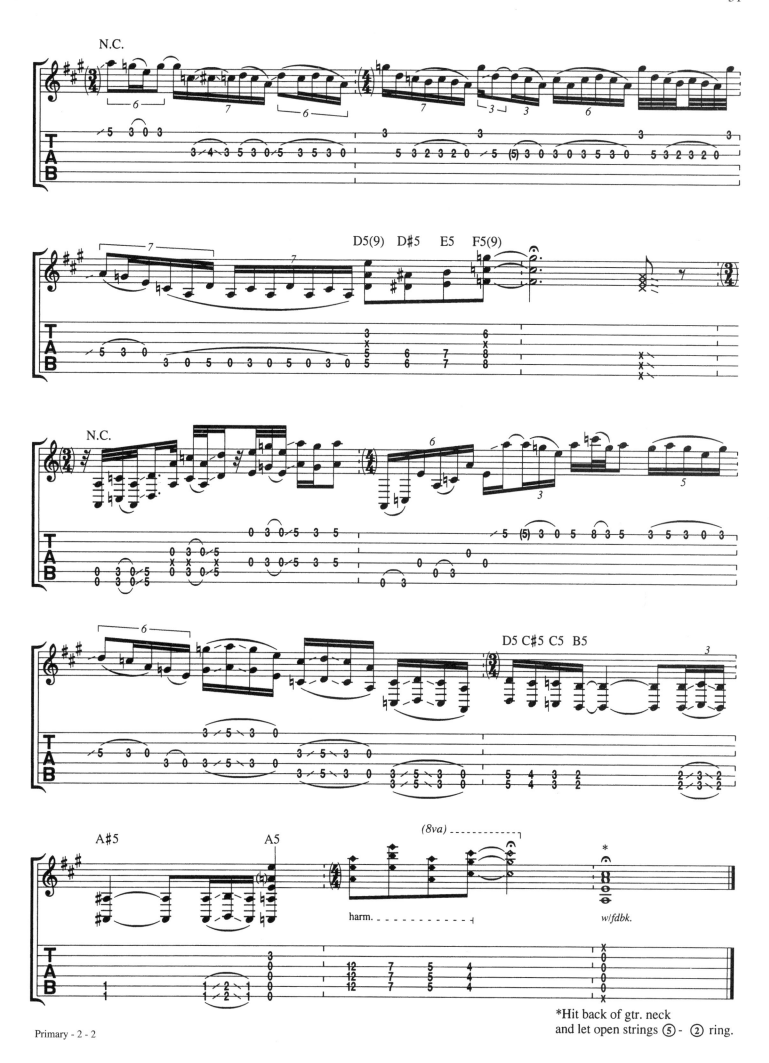

*Hit back of gtr. neck
and let open strings ⑤ - ② ring.

TORA! TORA!

Music by
EDWARD VAN HALEN, ALEX VAN HALEN,
MICHAEL ANTHONY and DAVID LEE ROTH

*Approx. 19 sec. With trem bar depressed,
randomly pick behind nut and hit slack
strings against fretboard to create rumble.

*Bend string
behind nut.

*Trill with L.H. and randomly tap
(sometimes tapping and sliding) with R.H.

Segue to LOSS OF CONTROL

GUITAR TAB GLOSSARY **

TABLATURE EXPLANATION

READING TABLATURE: Tablature illustrates the six strings of the guitar. Notes and chords are indicated by the placement of fret numbers on a given string(s).

String ⑥, 3rd Fret   String ① 12th Fret   A "C" Chord   C Chord Arpeggiated
                       String ③ 13th Fret

BENDING NOTES

HALF STEP: Play the note and bend string one half step.*

SLIGHT BEND (Microtone): Play the note and bend string slightly to the equivalent of half a fret.

BEND AND RELEASE: Play the note and gradually bend to the next pitch, then release to the original note. Only the first note is attacked.

WHOLE STEP: Play the note and bend string one whole step.

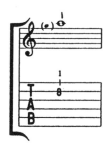

PREBEND (Ghost Bend): Bend to the specified note, before the string is picked.

BENDS INVOLVING MORE THAN ONE STRING: Play the note and bend string while playing an additional note (or notes) on another string(s). Upon release, relieve pressure from additional note(s), causing original note to sound alone.

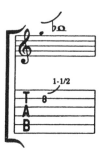

WHOLE STEP AND A HALF: Play the note and bend string a whole step and a half.

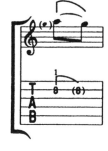

PREBEND AND RELEASE: Bend the string, play it, then release to the original note.

BENDS INVOLVING STATIONARY NOTES: Play notes and bend lower pitch, then hold until release begins (indicated at the point where line becomes solid).

TWO STEPS: Play the note and bend string two whole steps.

REVERSE BEND: Play the already-bent string, then immediately drop it down to the fretted note.

UNISON BEND: Play both notes and immediately bend the lower note to the same pitch as the higher note.

DOUBLE NOTE BEND: Play both notes and immediately bend both strings simultaneously.

*A half step is the smallest interval in Western music; it is equal to one fret. A whole step equals two frets.

© 1990 Beam Me Up Music
c/o CPP/Belwin, Inc. Miami, Florida 33014
International Copyright Secured   Made in U.S.A.   All Rights Reserved   **By Kenn Chipkin and Aaron Stang

RHYTHM SLASHES

STRUM INDICA-TIONS: Strum with indicated rhythm.

The chord voicings are found on the first page of the transcription underneath the song title.

INDICATING SINGLE NOTES USING RHYTHM SLASHES: Very often single notes are incorporated into a rhythm part. The note name is indicated above the rhythm slash with a fret number and a string indication.

ARTICULATIONS

HAMMER ON: Play lower note, then "hammer on" to higher note with another finger. Only the first note is attacked.

LEFT HAND HAMMER: Hammer on the first note played on each string with the left hand.

PULL OFF: Play higher note, then "pull off" to lower note with another finger. Only the first note is attacked.

FRET-BOARD TAPPING: "Tap" onto the note indicated by + with a finger of the pick hand, then pull off to the following note held by the fret hand.

TAP SLIDE: Same as fretboard tapping, but the tapped note is slid randomly up the fretboard, then pulled off to the following note.

BEND AND TAP TECHNIQUE: Play note and bend to specified interval. While holding bend, tap onto note indicated.

LEGATO SLIDE: Play note and slide to the following note. (Only first note is attacked).

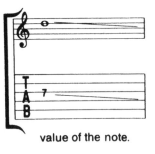

LONG GLISSAN-DO: Play note and slide in specified direction for the full value of the note.

SHORT GLISSAN-DO: Play note for its full value and slide in specified direction at the last possible moment.

PICK SLIDE: Slide the edge of the pick in specified direction across the length of the string(s).

MUTED STRINGS: A percussive sound is made by laying the fret hand across all six strings while pick hand strikes specified area (low, mid, high strings).

PALM MUTE: The note or notes are muted by the palm of the pick hand by lightly touching the string(s) near the bridge.

TREMOLO PICKING: The note or notes are picked as fast as possible.

TRILL: Hammer on and pull off consecutively and as fast as possible between the original note and the grace note.

ACCENT: Notes or chords are to be played with added emphasis.

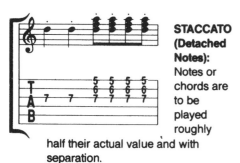

STACCATO (Detached Notes): Notes or chords are to be played roughly half their actual value and with separation.

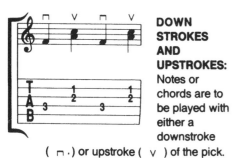

DOWN STROKES AND UPSTROKES: Notes or chords are to be played with either a downstroke (⊓ ·) or upstroke (∨) of the pick.

VIBRATO: The pitch of a note is varied by a rapid shaking of the fret hand finger, wrist, and forearm.

HARMONICS

NATURAL HARMONIC: A finger of the fret hand lightly touches the note or notes indicated in the tab and is played by the pick hand.

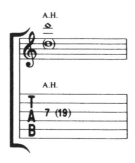

ARTIFICIAL HARMONIC: The first tab number is fretted, then the pick hand produces the harmonic by using a finger to lightly touch the same string at the second tab number (in parenthesis) and is then picked by another finger.

ARTIFICIAL "PINCH" HARMONIC: A note is fretted as indicated by the tab, then the pick hand produces the harmonic by squeezing the pick firmly while using the tip of the index finger in the pick attack. If parenthesis are found around the fretted note, it does not sound. No parenthesis means both the fretted note and A.H. are heard simultaneously.

TREMOLO BAR

SPECIFIED INTERVAL: The pitch of a note or chord is lowered to a specified interval and then may or may not return to the original pitch. The activity of the tremolo bar is graphically represented by peaks and valleys.

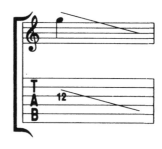

UN-SPECIFIED INTERVAL: The pitch of a note or a chord is lowered to an unspecified interval.